Soaring without an Engine

Parachutes, Gliders, and Hang Gliders

Contents

Written by Michele Paul

Introduction

Moving through the air without an engine for power may seem impossible unless you are a bird, but there are ways that people can do just that, both inside and outside planes.

People can be airborne outside an aircraft.

Special engineless planes, called gliders, enable people to use air currents rather than engines to move them through the air. For people who want the thrill of moving through the air outside an aircraft, hang gliders and parachutes allow them to move down to the ground from great heights.

Gliders

A glider looks like a plane and is made of light metal, fiberglass, or wood, and it also has some steel parts.

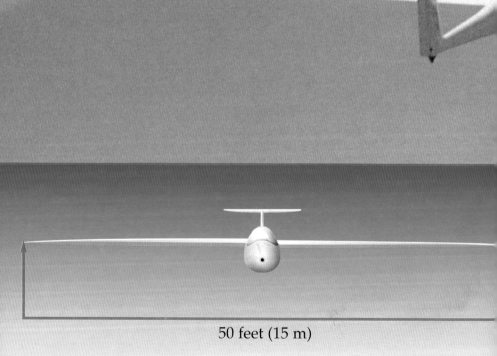

50 feet (15 m)

The wings of a glider are narrower than the wings of a plane. The glider wings can be about 50 feet (15 m) long and 3 feet (91 cm) wide. The wings are shaped like this to help the glider pilot use the air currents to fly. The pilot has controls for each wing so that the glider can be moved to the left and right.

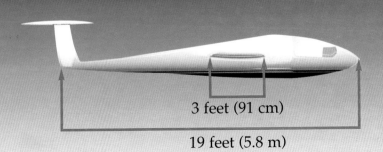

3 feet (91 cm)

19 feet (5.8 m)

The body of a glider gets narrower at the tail. The tail of a glider is made up of a stabilizer, an elevator, a fin, and a rudder. The glider pilot uses controls to move parts of the glider tail to help change direction.

Unlike planes, most gliders have only one wheel. This wheel and the landing equipment can move into the body of the glider when it is flying. Gliders have one or two seats.

Gliders can carry one or two people.

Launching Gliders

Before gliders can fly in the air, they have to be launched. Gliders can be launched in many ways.

By Small Glider Engine

Gliders can have engines so that they can be launched like a plane.

By Slingshot

Gliders can be shot into the air on bands. This is called shock-cord launching.

Launching Gliders

By Plane

Planes can tow gliders into the air.

By Winch

A winch on the ground can launch gliders.

By Car

Cars pull gliders along the ground until they soar into the air.

Flying Gliders

Once the glider is launched, it is released from whatever launched it, and begins its flight. Most glider flights last from one to five hours. Glider pilots have to be very skilled because they need to search for upward-moving air currents, called updrafts, to keep the glider airborne.

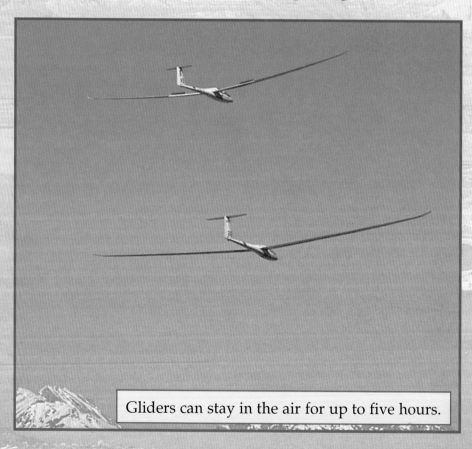

Gliders can stay in the air for up to five hours.

There are four kinds of updrafts that glider pilots look for. These are slope winds, thermals, mountain waves, and shear lines.

Slope winds or ridge currents	Winds that blow against a mountain or hill and are pushed up.
Thermals	Winds that rise upward after being warmed from heat on the ground.
Mountain waves	Air that sometimes occurs on the side of a mountain away from the wind.
Shear lines	Winds that occur when cool air moves into an area and forces warm air up.

If the pilot flies into an air current that is moving upward faster than the glider is going downward, the glider will go up. If the pilot does not find an upward-moving air current, the force of gravity will bring the glider back down to earth again.

History

The first glider was probably made in the early 1800s by George Cayley of England. In 1853, his coachman became the first person to fly in a glider but he had no control over the glider.

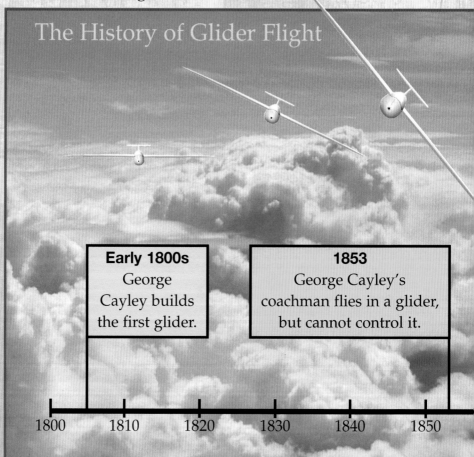

The History of Glider Flight

Early 1800s
George Cayley builds the first glider.

1853
George Cayley's coachman flies in a glider, but cannot control it.

1800   1810   1820   1830   1840   1850

In the late 1800s, Otto Lilienthal of Germany made many glider flights where he was able to control the glider. The first tow launch was in 1897. In the early 1900s, Orville and Wilbur Wright learned how to make a stable flight in a glider. The first known flight using slope winds to keep the glider up was made by Orville Wright.

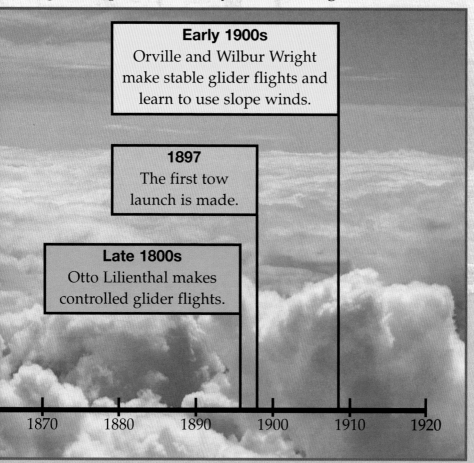

Early 1900s
Orville and Wilbur Wright make stable glider flights and learn to use slope winds.

1897
The first tow launch is made.

Late 1800s
Otto Lilienthal makes controlled glider flights.

1870   1880   1890   1900   1910   1920

Hang Gliders

Hang gliders are like big kites that people hang under. Unlike gliders, people operate hang gliders from outside the craft.

People hang beneath hang gliders.

Hang gliders have a large sail. The sail is usually triangular and is made out of fabric attached to a light metal frame. The frame is usually about 32 feet (9.8 m) wide. A harness hangs from the frame. The pilot is strapped into the harness and holds onto a control bar that hangs in front.

Like gliders, but unlike planes, hang gliders can carry only one or two people.

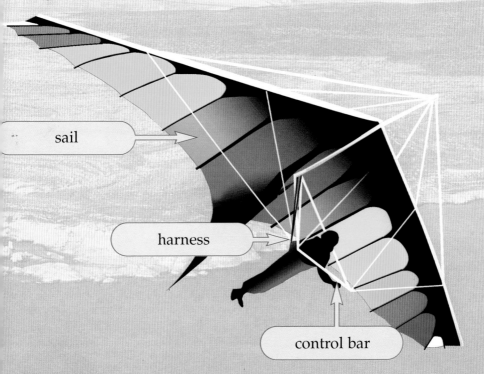

sail

harness

control bar

Launching Hang Gliders

As with gliders, there are different ways of launching a hang glider. Foot-launched gliding occurs when the pilot runs down the windward side of a hill, or launches from a cliff or mountain top.

People can run down a hillside to launch a hang glider.

Kiting, or tow-launched gliding, occurs when a hang glider is pulled into the air by a truck or boat. When the hang glider reaches about 400 feet (122 m), the towrope is released.

A hang glider after being launched.

Flying Hang Gliders

Like gliders, hang gliders can fly only if they are moving fast enough to keep air flowing past their wings. The hang-glider pilot searches for air currents that are moving upward, usually thermals.

A hang glider can move upward at a speed of 984 feet (300 m) per minute. The pilot moves the control bar to change the speed and direction of the hang glider by shifting his or her body.

A hang glider must move
fast enough to stay airborne.

History

Although there are records of hang-glider flights over a hundred years ago, it was in 1948 that a major development took place.

In that year a scientist, Francis Rogallo, developed flexible wings for hang gliders. These wings were unlikely to snap or break because of their flexibility. Earlier, flexible wings had only been used successfully on kites and model gliders.

An early hang glider

Parachutes

Unlike gliders and hang gliders, parachutes slow the fall of people or objects, usually from an aircraft.

Like gliders and hang gliders, parachutes are made up of several parts. These parts include a canopy, a harness, a bag, and straps.

The canopy is the part of a parachute that catches the air and slows down the fall. A modern canopy is usually a rectangular shape, made of up to 28 small panels, or gores.

Canopies used to be made of canvas, then silk, but are now made of nylon.

A canopy catches the air.

A parachutist wears a harness, which is strapped around their shoulders and legs. The harness has risers, or straps that connect to suspension lines. These suspension lines are attached to the canopy. The canopy stays inside a bag until the parachutist pulls a rip cord that releases it.

canopy

suspension lines

harness

A parachutist always carries a reserve parachute mounted just above the main parachute. The reserve parachute may save a parachutist's life if the main parachute does not open.

Parachutists go up in a plane to about 12,000 feet (3,658 m) and then they jump out. They wait for about three seconds to clear the plane before they pull the rip cord.

Parachutists jumping out of a plane.

The rip cord releases a small pilot parachute that helps open the main canopy.

pilot parachute

The main parachute will open after the pilot parachute.

The main canopy then fills with air and spreads out. This allows the parachutist to descend slowly to the ground. Parachutists descend at 17 feet (5.2 m) per second.

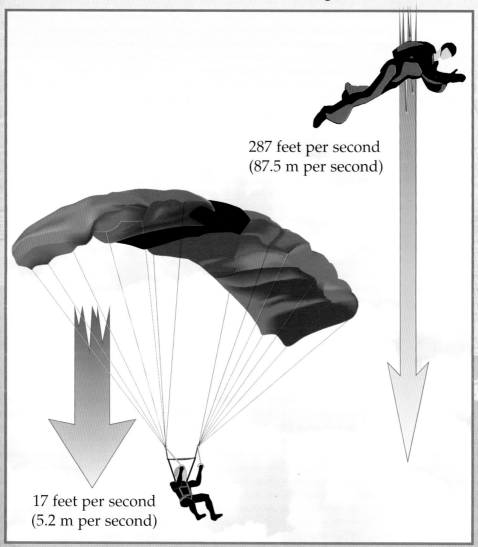

287 feet per second
(87.5 m per second)

17 feet per second
(5.2 m per second)

Parachutists are able to control their parachutes, like glider and hang-glider pilots can control their aircraft. Parachutists can turn right or left by pulling on steering lines, and can also control their speed.

steering line → ← steering line

History

Unlike gliders and hang gliders, parachutes have been around for hundreds of years. Leonardo da Vinci first suggested the idea of using a parachute about 500 years ago.

Early parachutists did not jump from planes because planes had not been invented. These early thrill seekers jumped from trees and towers.

This parachute was made from a drawing by Leonardo da Vinci.

Comparisons

Some of the same materials are used in the construction of gliders, hang gliders, and parachutes. Gliders are made of fiberglass, glass, light metal, and wire. Hang gliders are also made of light metal and wire, as well as fabric. Parachutes are made of fabric and nylon cord.

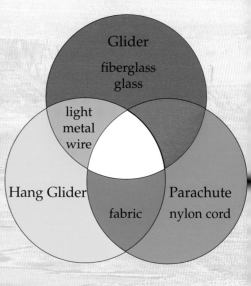

Glider

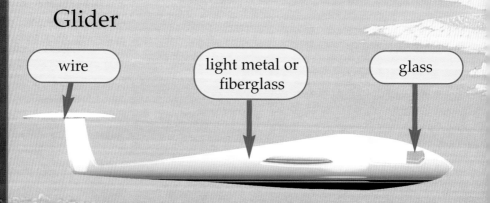

Hang Glider

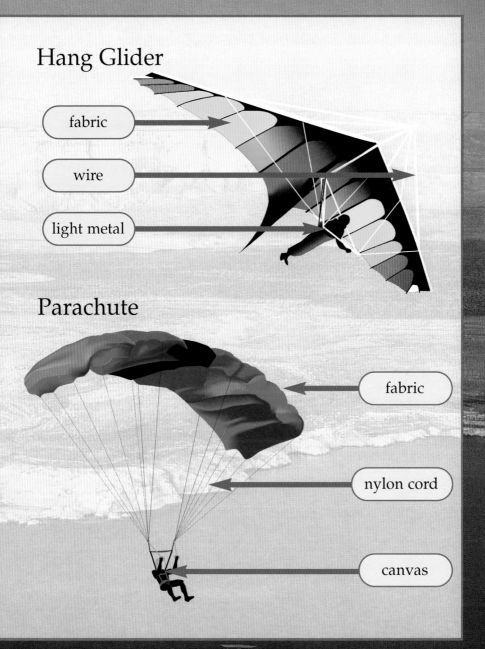

fabric

wire

light metal

Parachute

fabric

nylon cord

canvas

Comparing Gliders, Hang Gliders, and Parachutes

	Needs a motor to launch it	Has wing
Glider	✔	✔
Hang Glider	✗	✔
Parachute	✗	✗

lot inside	Is made of fiberglass	Opens in flight	Needs special weather conditions	Can carry more than one person
✔	✔	✗	✔	✔
✗	✗	✗	✔	✔
✗	✗	✔	✔	✔

✔ Yes
✗ No

29

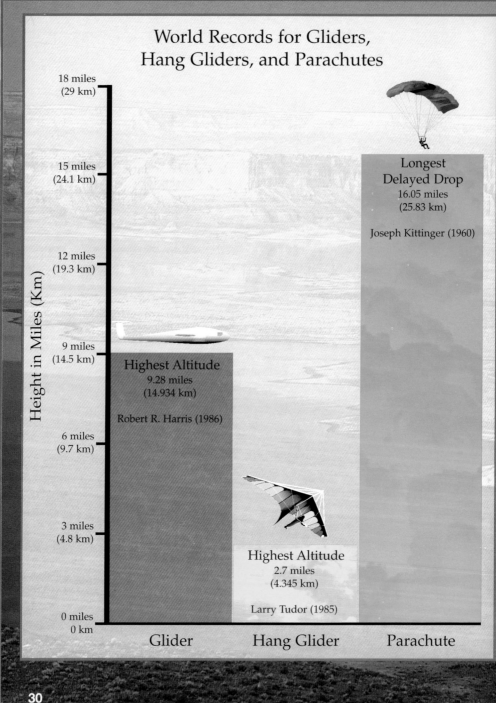

World Records for Gliders, Hang Gliders, and Parachutes

Height in Miles (Km)

18 miles (29 km)

15 miles (24.1 km)

12 miles (19.3 km)

9 miles (14.5 km)

6 miles (9.7 km)

3 miles (4.8 km)

0 miles
0 km

Longest
Delayed Drop
16.05 miles
(25.83 km)

Joseph Kittinger (1960)

Highest Altitude
9.28 miles
(14.934 km)

Robert R. Harris (1986)

Highest Altitude
2.7 miles
(4.345 km)

Larry Tudor (1985)

Glider   Hang Glider   Parachute